Let's Learn Urdu Using Pictures

Tasneem Raja M.A.(Eng.Lit.)

AuthorHouse™ UK Ltd.
1663 Liberty Drive
Bloomington, IN 47403 USA
www.authorhouse.co.uk
Phone: 0800.197.4150

Published by AuthorHouse 02/13/2014

ISBN: 978-1-4918-9381-4 (sc)
978-1-4918-9385-2 (e)

Any people depicted in stock imagery provided by Thinkstock are models,
and such images are being used for illustrative purposes only.
Certain stock imagery © Thinkstock.

This book is printed on acid-free paper.

authorHOUSE®

I AM CALLED 'ALIF MADD'

I LOOK LIKE AN:

 ARROW – JUST AS AN ARROW GOES UP, TAKE YOUR VOICE UP AND SAY 'AAH'

I DO NOT JOIN ON EITHER SIDE.

I STAND ALONE.

SOME OF MY WORDS ARE:

آم - AAM - MANGO

آپ - AAP - YOU

آج - AAJ - TODAY

I AM CALLED 'ALIF'

I LOOK LIKE AN:

ANT GOING UP - MY SOUND IS 'A' OR 'U'

I ONLY JOIN LETTERS WITH MY RIGHT HAND: ا

SOME OF MY WORDS ARE:

اب - UB - NOW

باپ - BAAP - DAD

جا - JA - GO

I AM CALLED 'BE'

I LOOK LIKE A:

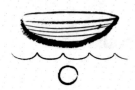

BUBBLE BENEATH A BOAT - SO MY SOUND IS 'B'

I HOLD HANDS ON BOTH SIDES.
WHEN USING ME, TAKE MY HEAD, LIKE THIS: بو
SOME OF MY WORDS ARE:

بادام - BADAM - ALMOND

بادل - BADAL - CLOUD

کباب - KEBAB

سبزی - SABZI - VEGETABLE

پ I AM CALLED A 'PE'

I LOOK LIKE A:

PODGY PANDA - SO MY SOUND IS 'P'

I JOIN ON BOTH SIDES TO USE ME, TAKE MY HEAD.

SOME OF MY WORDS ARE:

پاپا	- PAPA	-	DADDY
پانی	- PANI	-	WATER
چپ	- CHUP	-	QUIET
چپل	- CHAPPLE	-	SLIPPER

I AM CALLED 'TE'
(PUT YOUR TONGUE BEHIND YOUR FRONT TEETH).

I LOOK LIKE A:

TABLA DRUM - I AM A SOFT 'T'

I JOIN ON BOTH SIDES. WHEN YOU USE ME TAKE MY HEAD.
SOME OF MY WORDS ARE:

تتلی - TITLI - BUTTERFLY

تالا - TALA - LOCK

بارات - BARAT - WEDDING PARTY

ط ت
I AM CALLED 'TE'
(PUT YOUR TONGUE RIGHT BACK IN THE ROOF OF YOUR MOUTH).

I LOOK LIKE A:

TORTOISE - I AM A HARD 'T'

طر

I JOIN ON BOTH SIDES. TO USE ME, TAKE MY HEAD.
RECOGNISE ME FROM MY HEAD:

ٹوپی - TOPI - HAT

مٹر - MATTAR - PEA

چھپٹ لینا - CHAPAT LENA - TO SNATCH

 **I AM A 'SEY'**

I LOOK LIKE A:

SAIL - SO MY SOUND IS 'S'

I JOIN ON BOTH SIDES. RECOGNISE ME FROM MY SAIL.
SOME OF MY WORDS ARE:

ثمر - SUMR - FRUIT

مثلث - MUSALLAS - TRIANGLE

I AM CALLED A 'JEEM'

I LOOK LIKE A:

JUICY JUG - SO MY SOUND IS 'J'

I JOIN ON BOTH SIDES.
BUT YOU CAN ONLY SEE MY SPOUT AND DRIP:

جب	- JUB	- WHEN
بجلی	- BIJLI	- LIGHTNING
حج	- HAJJ	- PILGRIMAGE

I AM CALLED 'CHE'

I LOOK LIKE A:

CHERRY BUNCH - SO MY SOUND IS 'CH'

I JOIN ON BOTH SIDES, BUT YOU CAN RECOGNISE ME FROM MY LEAF
AND BERRIES.

SOME OF MY WORDS ARE:

چونچ - CHUNCH - BEAK

چاند - CHAND - MOON

I AM CALLED A 'HEY'

I LOOK LIKE A:

HEN - SO MY SOUND IS 'H'

I JOIN ON BOTH SIDES, BUT YOU CAN ONLY SEE MY HEAD.
SOME OF MY WORDS ARE:

حوصله - HAUSLA - COURAGE

حمله - HUMLA - ATTACK

صبح - SUBH - MORNING

(I only appear in Arabic loan words)

I AM CALLED A 'KHEY'

I LOOK LIKE A:

KHALIFA - SO MY SOUND IS 'KH'

I JOIN ON BOTH SIDES, BUT YOU CAN ONLY SEE MY MOUSTACHE AND EYE.

SOME OF MY WORDS ARE:

خط - KHAT - LETTER

فخر - FAKHAR - PRIDE

تلخ - TALKH - BITTER

I AM CALLED A 'THAL'

I LOOK LIKE:

SOMEONE POINTING OVER THERE - SO MY SOUND IS 'TH'

I ONLY HOLD HANDS ON MY RIGHT.
SOME OF MY WORDS ARE:

درد - THARTH - PAIN

دروازه - THARWAZA - DOOR

مرد - MARD - MAN

I AM CALLED A 'DAAL'

I LOOK LIKE A:

ڈ

DUCK - SO MY SOUND IS 'D'

I ONLY HOLD HANDS ON MY RIGHT.
SOME OF MY WORDS ARE:

ڈھونڈ - DHOOND - FIND

ڈبا - DABA - BOX

I AM CALLED A 'ZAAL'

I LOOK LIKE A:

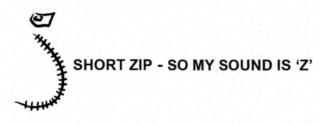

SHORT ZIP - SO MY SOUND IS 'Z'

I ONLY HOLD HANDS ON MY RIGHT.
SOME OF MY WORDS ARE:

ذائقہ - ZAIKA - TASTE

ذرا - ZARA - A LITTLE BIT

I AM CALLED A 'REY'

I LOOK LIKE A:

ROAD - SO MY SOUND IS 'R'

I ONLY HOLD HANDS ON MY RIGHT.
SOME OF MY WORDS ARE:

رس - RAS - JUICE

پرده - PARDAH - CURTAIN

I AM CALLED 'AREY'

I LOOK LIKE A:

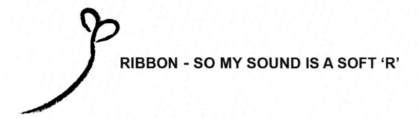

RIBBON - SO MY SOUND IS A SOFT 'R'

I ONLY JOIN ON MY RIGHT. BE CAREFUL WHEN YOU READ ME, SOMETIMES I LOOK LIKE THE LETTERS ر + ط , WHEN THEY ARE JOINED.

THERE IS ONLY ONE WORD WHICH BEGINS WITH ME:

روڑا - RORA - STONE

سڑک - SARK - ROAD

I AM CALLED A 'ZEY'

I LOOK LIKE A:

LONG ZIP - SO MY SOUND IS 'Z'

I ONLY HOLD HANDS ON MY RIGHT.
SOME OF MY WORDS ARE:

زیره - ZEERA - CUMIN

زیبائش - ZEBAISH - DECORATION

زمین - ZAMEEN - GROUND

(I am also the most common Z sound)

I AM CALLED A 'ZHEY'

I LOOK LIKE AN:

EXPLOSION - SO MY SOUND IS 'ZH'

I DO NOT APPEAR VERY OFTEN, AND THEN, ONLY IN
PERSIAN LOAN WORDS.
SOME OF MY WORDS ARE:

اژدها - AZHDHA - DRAGON

ژاله - ZHALA - HAIL, FROST

ژیغ ژیغ - ZHEGH ZHEGH - DROP-BY-DROP

I AM CALLED 'SEEN'

I LOOK LIKE THE:

SEA - SO MY SOUND IS 'S'

I JOIN LETTERS ON BOTH SIDES, BUT THEN YOU
ONLY USE MY WAVES. WHEN IAM REPEATED IN A WORD,
I TAKE A SPECIAL FORM, THUS: سسسس = سس

SOME OF MY WORDS ARE:

سر	-	SAR	-	HEAD
ساس	-	SAAS	-	MOTHER-IN-LAW
سرخ	-	SURKH	-	RED
سسر	-	SUSR	-	FATHER-IN-LAW

I AM CALLED 'SHEEN'

I LOOK LIKE A:

SHARK FIN - SO MY SOUND IS 'SH'

I JOIN ON BOTH SIDES. WHEN I AM REPEATED IN A WORD,
I TAKE A SPECIAL FORM, THUS: ثشر = ششر
SOME OF MY WORDS ARE:

شب	-	SHAB	- NIGHT
شترمرغ	-	SHUTR MURG	- OSTRICH
كشش	-	KASHASH	- ATTRACTION

I AM CALLED A 'SUAD'

I LOOK LIKE A:

SNAKE - SO MY SOUND IS A HEAVY 'S'

WHEN I JOIN ON BOTH SIDES, YOU CAN ONLY SEE MY HEAD.
SOME OF MY WORDS ARE:

صدى - SADI - CENTURY

تصویر - TASVEER - PICTURE

نقص - NUKS - DEFECT

I AM CALLED A 'ZUAD'

I LOOK LIKE A:

SNOOZING SNAKE - SO MY SOUND IS A HEAVY 'Z'

WHEN I JOIN ON BOTH SIDES, YOU CAN ONLY SEE MY SLEEPY HEAD.
SOME OF MY WORDS ARE:

ضعيف	-	ZAIF	-	OLD, WEAK
اضافه	-	IZAFA	-	INCREASE
بعض اوقات	-	BAAZ AUKAT	-	SOMETIMES

I AM CALLED 'TOAY'

I LOOK LIKE A:

TOILET - SO MY SOUND IS 'T' (HARD T)

I JOIN ON BOTH SIDES.
SOME OF MY WORDS ARE:

طاؤس - TAUS - PEACOCK

طلسم - TALSIM - MAGIC

خط - KHAT - LETTER

ظ I AM CALLED 'ZOAY'

I LOOK LIKE A:

GAZELLE - SO MY SOUND IS 'Z'

I JOIN ON BOTH SIDES.
SOME OF MY WORDS ARE:

فظول - FAZUL - USELESS

حفاظت - HIFAZAT - SAFETY

(I do not start very many words!)

I AM CALLED 'AIN'

I LOOK LIKE AN:

EAR - SO MY SOUND IS 'A'

WHEN I JOIN ON BOTH SIDES, I LOOK LIKE THIS:

AND ON THE END OF A WORD, I LOOK LIKE: ع

SOME OF MY WORDS ARE:

عقاب	-	AQAB	-	EAGLE
تعليم	-	TALEEM	-	EDUCATION
وسيع	-	VASI	-	SPACIOUS

I AM CALLED 'GHAIN'

I LOOK LIKE A:

 GHOST

I AM THE SAME IN FORM AS AIN.
SOME OF MY WORDS ARE:

غريب - GHAREEB - POOR

بغير - BAGHAIR - WITHOUT

فارغ - FARIGH - FREE

I AM CALLED 'FE'

I LOOK LIKE:

فِزّ

FIZZ - SO MY SOUND IS 'F'

I JOIN ON BOTH SIDES.
SOME OF MY WORDS ARE:

فرشته - FARISHTA - ANGEL

حفاظت - HIFAZAT - PROTECTION

برف - BARF - SNOW

I AM CALLED A 'QAAF'

I LOOK LIKE A:

KOALA - SO MY SOUND IS 'K'

I JOIN ON BOTH SIDES.
SOME OF MY WORDS ARE:

قصاب - QASSAB - BUTCHER

عقاب - AQAB - EAGLE

حق - HAQQ - RIGHT (n)

ک I AM CALLED 'KAAF'

I LOOK LIKE A:

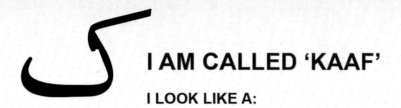

CANOE - SO MY SOUND IS 'K'

I JOIN ON BOTH SIDES, HOWEVER, WHEN I AM FOLLOWED BY
AN ALIF AND A LAAM, I TAKE A SPECIAL FORM.

SO ک + ا = کا ALSO ک + ل = کل

SOME OF MY WORDS ARE:

کمره - KAMRAH - ROOM

ملکیت - MILKIYAT - PROPERTY

ملک - MULK - COUNTRY

I AM CALLED A 'GAAF'

I LOOK LIKE A:

GOOSE - SO MY SOUND IS 'G'

I JOIN ON BOTH SIDES, AND LIKE KAAF, I TOO TAKE ON A SPECIAL FORM WHEN FOLLOWED BY ALIF AND LAAM.

SO گ + ا = گا ALSO گ + ل = گل

SOME OF MY WORDS ARE:

گدھا - GADHA - DONKEY

بگولا - BAGOLA - WHIRLWIND

امنگ - UMUNG - ASPIRATION

I AM CALLED 'LAAM'

I LOOK LIKE A:

 LADLE - SO MY SOUND IS 'L'

I JOIN ON BOTH SIDES - THIS IS HOW I DIFFER FROM ALIF, BECAUSE WE DO LOOK ALIKE.

WHEN I DO JOIN ON BOTH SIDES, YOU CAN ONLY SEE MY HANDLE.

I TOO HAVE A SPECIAL FORM FOR WHEN I JOIN WITH ALIF:

ل + ا = لا

SOME OF MY WORDS ARE:

لا ل	-	LAL	- RED
لڑکا	-	LARKA	- BOY
لفافه	-	LIFAFA	- ENVELOPE

I AM CALLED 'MEEM'

I LOOK LIKE A:

LITTLE MOUSE - SO MY SOUND IS 'M'

I AM A FRIENDLY MOUSE, AND WHEN I JOIN ON BOTH SIDES, YOU CAN ONLY SEE MY BODY.

SOME OF MY WORDS ARE:

مٹر - MATTAR - PEA

کمرہ - KAMRAH - ROOM

کام - KAM - WORK

I AM CALLED 'NOON'

I LOOK LIKE A:

     NOSE - SO MY SOUND IS 'N'

I JOIN ON BOTH SIDES.

SOME OF MY WORDS ARE:

ناشپاتی - NASHPATI - PEAR

جنوب - JUNOOB - SOUTH

تین - TEEN - THREE

I AM CALLED A 'VOW'

I DON'T LOOK LIKE ANYTHING, BUT THE LETTERS OF MY NAME

TELL WHAT I DO:

V - I SOMETIMES HAVE A V SOUND

O - I ACT AS VOWEL 'OO'

W - I HAVE A W SOUND

I ONLY JOIN ON MY RIGHT.

SOME OF MY WORDS ARE:

والدین	- VALDEN	-	PARENTS
روڑا	- RORA	-	STONE
دو	- THO	-	TWO

I AM CALLED A 'DO KASHMI HE'

I LOOK LIKE A:

BROKEN HEART - SO WHEN YOU SAY ME, SIGH GENTLY!

I ONLY ACCENT A CONSONANT, I JOIN ON BOTH SIDES.
SOME OF MY WORDS ARE:

بھائی - BHAI - BROTHER

پھر - PHIR - THEN

ه

I AM CALLED 'HEY'

I AM THE MOST COMMON 'H' SOUND - BUT BECAUSE I HAVE SO MANY
DIFFERENT FORMS, I AM COMPLICATED.

THIS IS HOW I LOOK:

IN THE BEGINNING - I LOOK LIKE A HAIR CURL	هـ
IN THE MIDDLE - I AM WAVY HAIR	ـهـ
IN THE END - I AM WAVY OR CURLY	ـه

I JOIN ON BOTH SIDES.
SOME OF MY WORDS ARE:

ہاتھی	- HATI	-	ELEPHANT
پہنچنا	- POHUNCHNA	-	TO ARRIVE
تکیہ	- TAKEA	-	PILLOW
کمرہ	- KAMRA	-	ROOM

36

 **I AM CALLED 'CHOTI (SMALL) YEH'**

I LOOK LIKE:

　　　　　A MOUTH SAYING 'EEEEEH'

WHEN YOU SEE ME AT THE END OF A WORD, SAY 'CH 'EEEE' SE'!
IN THE MIDDLE OF A WORD, I LOOK LIKE

　AND AT THE START:

I JOIN ON BOTH SIDES. I ACT LIKE THE LETTER Y.
SOME OF MY WORDS ARE:

يتيم	-	YATIM	- ORPHAN
ياسمين	-	YASMIN	- JASMIN
بلّى	-	BILLI	- CAT

I AM CALLED 'BUREE (BIG) YEH'

I LOOK LIKE AN:

 ELBOW

WHEN YOU SEE ME AT THE END OF WORDS, SAY 'EH' FOR ELBOW -
LIKE MY BROTHER, I ALSO HAVE THE BEGINNING / MIDDLE FORMS OF:

 &

I JOIN ON BOTH SIDES. I ACT LIKE THE LETTER Y.
SOME OF MY WORDS ARE:

يتيم - YATIM - ORPHAN

نيچے - NEECHE - UNDER

ہے - HAI - IS

THE DIFFERENCE IN SOUND BETWEEN THE TWO YEH'S IS ONLY APPARENT
WHEN THEY APPEAR AT THE END OR IN THE MIDDLE,
DEPENDING UPON THE WORD.
WHEN AT THE BEGINNING, BOTH HAVE THE SAME SOUND OF Y.

WHEN IN THE MIDDLE AND AT THE END OF WORDS, THE SOUND SHOULD
READ 'EH' OR 'EE'.

FOR EXAMPLE, THIS DIFFERENCE CAN BE ILLUSTRATED AS FOLLOWS:

میں - MAIN - I

میں - MEIN - IN

میری - MEREE - MY

I AM CALLED 'NOON GUNNA'

I AM AN ACCENT, NOT A LETTER IN MY OWN RIGHT - I ONLY APPEAR

AT THE END OF WORDS - I AM A NASAL 'N' SOUND.

SOME OF MY WORDS ARE:

میں	-	MEIN	- ME / I
کیوں	-	KYON	- WHY?
ہیں	-	HAIN	- ARE
ہوں	-	HUN	- AM

ACCENTS

URDU LETTERS ARE MADE UP OF CONSONANTS AND VOWELS.

THE VOWELS ARE: آ , ا , ع , و , ی , ے .

THESE ARE CALLED LONG VOWELS, BECAUSE THEY
ELONGATE THEIR SOUND.
HOWEVER, IN URDU, THERE ARE ALSO SHORT
VOWELS / ACCENTS. THE SOUND IS SHORTER AND TIGHTER:

1	اَ	ZABAR	-	U / A
2	اِ	ZER	-	E
3	اُ	PESH	-	O
4	اً	DOUBLE ZABAR	-	UN
5	اّ	TASHADAD	-	DOUBLE SAY THE MARKED CONSONANT.

FINALLY, WE HAVE ء - HAMZA. THIS ACCENT HAS AN 'A' SOUND
AND HELPS JOIN TWO VOWELS E.G.

| بھائی | - | BHAI | - | BROTHER |
| لئے | - | LIYE | - | FOR |

WHEN WE BEGIN WRITING – WE BASICALLY TAKE THE HEAD OF THE
LETTER AND JOIN IT DIRECT TO THE NEXT HEAD. WHEN YOU WRITE URDU
THE DIRECTION FLOWS FROM RIGHT TO LEFT.
USUALLY, LETTERS AT THE END OF A WORD ARE IN THEIR FULL FORM.
IF THE CHARACTERS CAN JOIN, THEY SHOULD. IF THEY CANNOT THEN
THEY DO NOT.

SO LETS WRITE KITAB   ک + ت + ا + ب   کتاب =

SO WE WOULD JOIN: ک + ﺘ + ﺎ + ب

MEIN   ں + م + ے = میں

NASHPATI   = ن + ا + ش + پ + ا + ت + ی   ناشپاتی

GAJAR   ر + ج + ا + گ = گاجر

THARAKHT   ت + خ + ر + د = درخت

REMEMBER: URDU IS NOT A LINEAR LANGUAGE – THE FLOW OF THE
WRITING IS ALMOST SLANTING DOWNWARDS LIKE THESE ARROWS ↙ ↙

WRITE THESE WORDS IN JOINT FORM:

ت + ک + ی + ه   (PILLOW)

ک + س + ا + ن   (FARMER)

م + ق + ا + م + ی   (LOCAL)

ع + و + ا + م   (PUBLIC)

س + ر + ک + ا + ر + ی   (OFFICIAL)

ب + ا + ه + ر   (OUTSIDE)

ا + س + ت + ق + ب + ا + ل   (RECEPTION)

و + ر + ز + ش   (EXERCISE)

ص + ح + ت   HEALTH)

ک + ا + غ + ز   (PAPER)

د + ر + م + ی + ا + ن   (BETWEEN)

ت + ر + ق + ی   (PROGRESS)

س + ت + ا + ر + ه   (STAR)

ح + ج + ا + ب   (HIJAB)

م + ض + ب + و + ط   (STRONG)

ص + ا + ف   (CLEAN)

خ + و + ش (HAPPY)

خ + و + ب + ص + و + ر + ت (BEAUTIFUL)

ذ + ی + ب + ا + ء + ش (ORNAMENT)

ل + ی + م + و + ں (LEMON)

م + ز + ا + ح + ی + ہ (FUNNY)

گ + ه + و + ن + س + ل + ا (NEST)

ق + ی + ن + چ + ی (SCISSORS)

س + ڑ + ک (ROAD)

ب + ه + ا + ء + ی (BROTHER)

ض + ر + و + ر + ی (NECESSARY)

د + س + ت + ی + ا + ب (AVAILABLE)

ا + و + س + ط (AVERAGE)

م + س + ت + ق + ل (PERMANENT)

ت + صّ + و + ر (IMAGINATION)

و + س + ا + ء + ل (RESOURCES)

44

ڈ + ک + ا + ٹ + ر   (DOCTOR)

چ + ل + ا + ل   (GREED)

ح + ی + ح + ص   (CORRECT)

ی + گ + د + و + ل + آ   (POLLUTION)

ش + خ + ص + ی + ت   (PERSONALITY)

اُ + ق + ا + ف + ت + ا   (BY CHANCE)

بُ + ھ + ر + پ + و + رُ   (OVERFLOWING)

س + و + ر + ج   (SUN)

ت + ع + ل + ی + م   (EDUCATION)

ک + ھ + ا + ن + ا   (DINNER)

چ + ھ + ت + ر + ی   (UMBRELLA)

ہ + ے   (IS)

ہ + ے + ں   (ARE)

ہ + و + ں   (AM)

ج + ا + ن + ا   (TO GO)

ر + ہ + ن + ا   (TO LIVE /STAY)

Printed in the United States
By Bookmasters